WORLD IN CRISIS

THE RACE TO FIX THE
GLOBAL
ECONOMY

Sarah Levete

rosen publishing's
rosen
central®

NEW YORK

Published in 2015 by The Rosen Publishing Group, Inc.
29 East 21st Street
New York, NY 10010

Copyright © 2015 by The Rosen Publishing Group, Inc.

First Edition

Produced for Rosen by Calcium Creative Ltd.
Editor for Calcium Creative Ltd.: Sarah Eason
Designer: Paul Myerscough
Picture research: Rachel Blount

Library of Congress Cataloging-in-Publication Data

Levete, Sarah.
The race to fix the global economy/Sarah Levete.—First Edition.
    pages cm.—(World in crisis)
Audience: Grades 7–12.
Includes bibliographical references and index.
ISBN 978-1-4777-7844-9 (library bound)
1. Globalization—Economic aspects—Juvenile literature. 2. Financial crises—Juvenile literature. 3. International finance—Juvenile literature. I. Title.
HF1359.L43648 2015
337—dc23

                                        2014003041

Manufactured in Malaysia

Photo credits: Cover: Dreamstime:Americanspirit; Inside: Dreamstime:Americanspirit 40, Darren Baker 26, Sam D\'cruz 24, Igor Dolgov 35, Dreammediapeel 13, Julie Feinstein 42, Lonny Garris 37, Gawriloff 7, Tomas Hajek 41, Lindaparton 33, Lucidwaters 44, Monkey Business Images 30, Soleg1974 6, Tbe 19, Tissizis John 5, Kheng Ho Toh 45, Tupungato 16, Vclements 9, Konstantin Yuganov 31; Shutterstock:AlexKol Photography 8, Radu Bercan 4, 11, Blend Images 10, Andy Dean Photography 20, 28, Eyeidea 22, Fpolat69 23, Fstockfoto 17, ID1974 34, Jag CZ 12, Joyfull 39, Ramona Kaulitzki 15, Daryl Lang 18, Lewis Tse Pui Lung 27, Tatiana Morozova 25, Paintings 38, Lucia Pitter 14, Portokalis 32, SSSCCC 36; Wikimedia Commons: Dorothea Lange, Farm Security Administration/Office of War Information/Library of Congress 43, David Shankbone 29, World Telegram staff photographer/Library of Congress 21.

Contents

The Economy in Crisis

The twenty-first century: we make robots that respond to our commands. We send men and women up into space, and down to the depths of the ocean. Despite these amazing achievements, we do not seem to manage our economies very well. Countries run out of money. Parts of the United States Federal Government shut down because of debt. Banks collapse. Investors lose all their money. Businesses fold and people lose their jobs. All these events are linked to the global economy.

The strength or weakness of the global economy can influence the success of many businesses, from small stores to large malls.

What Is the Economy?

The economy is made up of the jobs we do, the products we make, the services we offer, the money we earn, and how we spend and save that money. Countries, cities, towns, big businesses, small businesses, and families all have their own economies. A government is responsible for its nation's economy, and this affects the economies of businesses, both large and small, which in turn influence those of families and individuals.

The term "global economy" refers to the way that the economies in the world link together. No single country or continent is responsible for the global economy.

Economy Is Everything

The economy has an effect on basic human needs and/or rights, such as having a nutritious diet, getting access to health care, and receiving a good education. It is about being able to get a job and affording enough food, clothes, and some luxuries. The economy affects everyone, from a wealthy banker in a developed country to a farmer trying to sell his or her crops in a developing country.

COUNTDOWN!

The global economy has reached crisis point before. In the 1930s, the world was plunged into economic hardship by the Great Depression that followed the collapse of the U.S. financial markets in 1929. Even now some developed countries such as Greece and Portugal are struggling to recover from the economic crisis that gripped the world in 2008.

When the global economy collapses, jobs are lost, families struggle to pay their bills, people riot in the streets, and governments change. Can the global economy be fixed or is the next economic crisis just around the corner?

CHAPTER ONE

Understanding the Global Economy

Stores stock a huge number of different products for us to buy. Many of these will have been partly or wholly made in other countries, such as China, India, Thailand, and Germany. Computers, smart phones, and cars are made from parts that are produced around the world. This process is made possible by the workings of the global economy, which involves many activities across the world, including earning and borrowing money, and importing and exporting goods.

Money, Income, and Debt

Money is a type of currency. Currency moves around a country, and between countries, which allows people and businesses to buy what they need. We know money mostly as coins, bills, and credit cards, although anything can be used as currency, as long as people agree on the value the currency represents.

The purchase and sale of goods is a key part of the economy. Without the import and export of goods, the world economy could not operate effectively.

Money takes many forms, from coins and notes to plastic cards. Money also exists as entries on bank records or online transactions.

The money that comes into a household, business, or even government, is called income. Expenditure is what is spent. If we spend more money than we earn, we are in debt. The economic crisis in the early twenty-first century was partly caused by the massive amounts of debt that banks built up.

Buying and Selling

We use money to buy goods and services. Goods are items such as food and cars that are made, transported to a store or other outlet, and sold. Services are not physical products that people can hold. They are things that people provide, such as education or health care, and hairdressing or sports coaching. The person or company that buys goods or services is the consumer. The person or company that makes the goods or provides the service is the producer.

The exchange of goods or services for money, or exchanging them for other goods or services, is called a trade. If a person buys a T-shirt from a store, it is a trade—the consumer pays money to the seller who probably bought the T-shirt from the producer. If a person swaps a T-shirt for a computer game with a friend it is also a trade.

LOOK TO THE PAST

Before there was money, people swapped one thing for another in an exchange called bartering. If a farmer had corn but wanted a cow, he could barter his corn for a cow, after first agreeing how much corn the cow was worth. When goods such as crops were traded over large distances, bartering became more difficult to manage.

The ability to ship goods across oceans transformed the amount of trade between nations.

In the Beginning

The global economy began to take shape in the late-eighteenth and nineteenth centuries. This was a time of rapid invention and discovery, scientific advance, and technological innovation. The period, known as the Industrial Revolution, began in Britain and later took hold in the United States. New methods of production, power, and transport changed the face of agriculture and industry in many countries across the world.

Full Steam Ahead!

Around 1764, the Scottish inventor James Watt developed a new, improved steam engine, and soon steam was powering industry and transport. Steam engines began to replace water as the driving force behind industry, meaning that factories could be built anywhere and not just near a water supply. Watt's invention helped speed up production, and made transportation quicker and more efficient.

Product Power

During the nineteenth century, industrial products were produced using steam or coal power. After the world's first large electrical generating station opened in Niagara Falls, United States, in 1895, it became possible to transmit power over long distances. Such technological changes enabled factories to produce goods on a much larger scale. Electricity in factories meant they could manufacture goods day and night. The economy expanded as business and trade thrived.

A Transportation Revolution

Developments in transportation revolutionized society. Large steam ships could carry raw materials across oceans. Railways could move goods quickly over long distances, and refrigerated transport made it possible to carry perishable goods even farther. With the use of aircraft, trade was transformed as the movement of goods became even quicker and more reliable.

Keeping the Money Rolling

As trade increased, traders wanted to borrow money to expand or develop their businesses. Workers needed to be paid and raw materials had to be bought. Banks, which had existed long before the Industrial Revolution, provided this support, and money began to flow around the economy.

SCIENCE SOLUTIONS

Internet Revolution

Steam power transformed the world's economies 200 years ago, allowing goods to be mass-produced and shipped around the globe. Much more recently, the Internet sparked a new revolution in the global economy. Companies and individuals could now communicate online and in real time, managing businesses and trading anywhere in the world at the click of a mouse.

Today's Global Economy

The global economy never sleeps. Every minute of the day, trucks, ships, and aircraft crisscross the globe, carrying a vast range of products, from bananas to shampoo, and computers to motorcycles. The global economy links continents, countries, businesses, and individuals all over the world. Without it, society as we know it would grind to a halt.

The Domino Effect

Different countries depend on each other for trade and business. This system works well when it runs smoothly. However, when there is a problem with the economy in one country, it can cause a problem in a country on the other side of the world, leading to further difficulties for small businesses and individuals everywhere. The effect is a little like watching a row of dominoes crash down, one by one.

Rich and Poor

There is no exact way to measure the wealth of one country against that of another. However, many people judge a nation's overall wealth by looking at its Gross Domestic Product (GDP) per person.

The global economy links countries and nations across the world. It is a web of financial activity.

GDP is roughly the value of all the goods and services produced by a country over a year, divided by the country's population. The GDP per person of Qatar, a developed country in the Middle East, is $105,000, whereas the Democratic Republic of Congo, a developing country in Africa, has a GDP per person of less than $400. Developed countries have a strong influence in the global economy because their money and trade helps keep it active. Developing countries have less influence and often suffer most hardship as a result of global economic problems.

From Local to Global

Many businesses are owned by an even bigger business. Some large companies, called multinationals, have businesses, factories, and offices in many different countries. Extremely large companies such as Coca-Cola are multinationals.

The concentrated ingredients used to make Coca-Cola are exported to more than 900 bottling plants around the world. The drink is then sold in more than 200 countries.

SCIENCE SOLUTIONS

Fragile Network

It can be incredibly difficult to untangle the complex web of companies around the world and find out who owns what. However, a recent study by the University of Zurich analyzed more than 43,000 multinational corporations and made a complex web of the 1,318 companies at the heart of the global economy. The researchers found that an even smaller network of 147 companies controlled 40 percent of the whole global economy. If any companies in that network collapsed, the global economy could be seriously affected.

Global Trading

Without a global economy, there would be many things we could not enjoy whenever we want—like a pizza. A pizza contains a variety of ingredients that probably come from many different countries. The trading and transport of those ingredients is made possible only by the global economy.

What Is Trade?

Today, most countries trade with other countries. They sell or export goods to other countries, and buy in or import goods and services from other countries. This back and forth exchange keeps money flowing between countries. However, trading around the globe puts pressure on businesses that have to compete with many other businesses and companies offering similar goods. In order to make money or a profit, businesses try to lower the cost of making goods at the same time as making more goods to trade. This can cause problems. The quality of the goods may be reduced, and, more importantly, the safety and well-being of workers may be overlooked.

Supply and Demand

The price of goods often depends upon supply and demand. The supply is the availability of goods, and the demand is the number of people wanting to buy the goods. The balance between supply and demand can have a huge impact on the economy of a business or a country, and the global economy. For instance, the United States

The olives in a pizza may have come from Greece, the tomatoes from Spain, and the wheat base from American farms. The end product relies on ingredients that have been bought from various countries.

and Britain trade in many different goods and services. If consumers in the United States spend less on British goods, then export businesses in Britain will make less money. The British businesses may then reduce the amount of goods that they produce and even reduce the number of people they employ. If there are more unemployed people with less to spend, the British economy dips.

LOOK TO THE PAST

No one can control natural disasters, and they can have a serious effect on global trading and the global economy. According to the United Nations (UN), the Japanese car manufacturer Toyota lost $1.2 billion in 2011 because essential car parts could not be provided after the major earthquake and tsunami that hit Japan that year. This, in turn, affected other countries with Toyota factories. In the United States, 150,000 fewer cars were manufactured, and car production fell 70 percent in India and 50 percent in China.

CHAPTER TWO

Money Makes the World Go Round

Money is at the heart of the economy. Businesses want to make a profit so that they have an income and can grow into bigger businesses. When they trade globally, businesses have to overcome the obstacle of different countries using different kinds of money, or currencies.

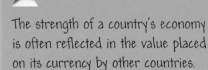

The strength of a country's economy is often reflected in the value placed on its currency by other countries.

Working with Different Currencies

When people travel abroad, they first need to buy some of the other country's currency so that they have money to spend. A bank exchanges U.S. dollars for paper money or coins in the foreign currency. How much people get for their U.S. dollars depends on the exchange rate. This is how much one currency is worth in relation to another currency. Exchange rates can go up and down for various reasons, including what people think about a country's economy and any political issues that may affect the country.

A country's rate of exchange rises and falls depending on whether other countries think its economy is doing well or struggling. Before people put money into a business, they will first look at the economy and exchange rate in that business's country to make sure that it is a safe investment.

A Single Currency

In Europe, a number of countries have combined to create a single currency—the Euro—to make it easier for them to trade with each other. The countries belong to an organization called the European Union (EU). The organization's origins go back to the years after World War II when politicians wanted to bind Europe together in the hope there would never be a repeat of such a war. In 2002, the majority of EU countries switched their currency to the Euro, although some countries, including Britain, refused to join and kept their own currency.

Seven percent of the world's population lives in the EU, but the EU's trade with the rest of the world makes up 20 percent of global exports and imports.

LOOK TO THE PAST

In the sixteenth century, silver was the currency of choice. For about 200 years, silver was extremely valuable. However, so much silver was dug from silver mines that it began to lose its value. In the same way, simply printing more money does not correct economic problems—the money just loses its value.

Banks are global businesses that often run financial operations in many countries.

The World of Banks

When someone gets a job and starts to earn money, he or she will probably open a bank account to keep that money safe. Banking is a global industry. There are thousands of banks around the world making sure that money can pass from person to person, business to business, and country to country. The banking industry enables money to flow around the world.

Banks for Everyone?

Some banks operate on their own. Others are owned by larger banks. Individuals and small businesses usually put their money in retail banks, which have many separate offices, or branches, that people can visit, sometimes in more than one country. Big companies and wealthy individuals use investment banks to look after their money. The business of all banks, whatever their size or type, is money and making a profit.

A Global Bank

The World Bank, founded in 1944, is made up of more than 180 member countries. It earns money by making investments and charging fees to its members. The bank's aim is to encourage strong economies and reduce world poverty.

Central Banks

Most countries have a central bank that looks after the government's money and creates the bills and coins that make up a nation's currency. The United States central bank is the Federal Reserve. Every day, a country's banks have to deposit a certain amount of money in the central bank. Central banks lend money to banks when no one else will. This is called "acting as the lender of last resort."

LOOK TO THE PAST

After the Great Depression in the 1930s, the United States took steps to prevent such a crisis from happening again by introducing a law called the Glass-Steagall Act. This law made sure that investment banks and retail banks operated independently, to protect an individual's savings, and to prevent banks from becoming too large and uncontrollable. In 1999, the two types of bank were once again allowed to link activities, which led to large banks taking financial risks. These risks contributed to the global economic meltdown that began in 2007.

A central bank, such as the Federal Reserve, influences its nation's economy by altering interest rates and managing the country's supply of credit and money.

Lend and Spend

Banks need to make money so they can pay their expenses and make a profit. To make money, banks must do something with the money that people hand over to them. The banks either lend this money to other people, or they invest it so it can earn more money. When we put money into a bank as savings, the bank promises to pay interest, which is extra money added to the invested money. When we borrow money from a bank, it charges interest on that amount, which is some money added to the loan. We then have to pay back the loan and the interest. The percentage the bank decides to add to the amount saved or borrowed is called the interest rate. Interest rates go up and down, depending on what is happening in both a country's economy and the global economy.

Taking a Share

When banks invest money, they often buy parts, or shares, of companies or organizations, expecting those companies or organizations to be profitable. When a company does well, the value of the shares rises. If it does not do well, the value of the shares falls. Investment bankers try to buy shares when the price is low and sell them when the price is high, so they make as much profit as possible. There is no guarantee that an investment will make money—it is a risk. In the global economy, shares can be bought and sold by companies and individuals thousands of miles away from each other.

The New York Stock Exchange is one of the most famous stock exchanges in the world. Shares in companies are traded at stock exchanges.

Lending Big

When a government or a big company needs to borrow very large amounts of money, it can issue "bonds." When someone buys a bond, he or she is really lending money to the issuer of the bond. In return for the loan, or purchase of the bond, the issuer pays a fixed rate of interest and promises to pay back the original amount loaned at an agreed date. Investors buy and sell bonds to make money.

COUNTDOWN!

It is not always easy to know where a bank invests our money. It might choose to invest it in an oil company, which then invests in another company that might be involved in making weapons that find their way to terrorists. People are becoming more concerned about where their money is invested and turning increasingly to "ethical banks," which invest in projects that benefit the environment and other good causes.

CHAPTER THREE

What Could Possibly Go Wrong?

There are many advantages to a global economy, but it can also create plenty of problems. When one country experiences difficulties in its economy or banking system, there is often a ripple effect across the world. In recent years, there have been severe crises in the world economy that have seen governments topple, banks go bankrupt, and countries run out of money.

The mortgage crisis in the United States triggered global economic unrest.

Boom and Bust

In a strong economy, people have jobs and spend money, businesses and investors make more money, and banks lend money. In a weak economy, people lose their jobs and spend less, businesses lose money, no one wants to invest, and banks stop lending. In the 1990s, the U.S. and British economies were booming—and then they went bust.

The Mortgage Crisis

A mortgage is a large loan to buy a home. The borrower pays back a part of the loan each month with interest charged on top. During a period of boom in the early twenty-first century, banks in the United States began to offer loans to people who were on low incomes. The banks offered low interest rates so, at first, repayments were quite small. However, when interest rates rose, people were unable to afford the higher repayments. They had to hand their homes back to the banks, which were then unable to sell the homes because no one could afford to buy them. Meanwhile, banks had "sold" the mortgages to other banks and companies around the world. When one bank lost money, so did all the others involved in the complex chain of selling and buying loans.

LOOK TO THE PAST

In the 1920s, the U.S. economy was booming. However, there were problems ahead. Following the end of World War I in 1918, European farmers started to grow more food and so bought fewer U.S. exports. Advances in farming technology increased the amount of produce, which led to lower food prices. The same thing happened in other industries, such as coal and shipbuilding. People who had shares in U.S. companies began to sell them, and their value dropped. Other people then tried to sell their shares, but no one wanted to buy them. In October 1929, the New York Wall Street stock market crashed. Banks closed their doors, and people lost their savings. A long period of unemployment and poverty—the Great Depression—followed.

Economic Influences

What makes an economy healthy or weak? There are many influences, from the discovery of resources such as oil and gas to natural disasters and civil war. Politics— how a country is governed—also affects the way the economy is run, what is spent, and what is borrowed. For example, some countries spend a lot of money on public services such as health care and education. They raise the money for this from high taxes. Other countries raise less money from taxes and might expect people to pay for their own health care.

Hungry for Energy

From transport to Internet use, almost everything we do requires fuel or electricity that comes from natural energy sources, particularly oil and natural gas. Price increases in oil and natural gas have a ripple effect on the prices of other goods and services around the world. If prices rise but incomes do not, people will have less discretionary income and so will spend less on goods and services. This can have a serious effect on a country's economy.

This oil rig is used to extract fossil fuel oil from the seabed. The supply and demand of fossil fuels continues to influence the global economy.

War and Unrest

If a country is in turmoil or at war, its economy suffers. Foreign investors are likely to consider the country too risky to invest in, and even everyday trading becomes difficult. In 2011, the uprising known as the Arab Spring saw social and political unrest in several Middle Eastern and North African countries such as Tunisia and Egypt. In Syria, a terrible civil war began, not only killing thousands of civilians and destroying towns and cities, but also ruining the economy because businesses were unable to operate in the disruption. Many countries refused to import oil from Syria because they did not want to support the rulers of the country.

Syria's economy has been devastated by prolonged conflict and war.

COUNTDOWN!

War between political parties can also bring a country's economy to its knees. In 2013, bitter arguments between the Republican and Democratic parties in the United States led to parts of the Federal Government shutting down for a number of weeks. Parks and museums were closed, and employees were sent home. Part of the infighting was over President Obama's health care policy, which Republicans did not want to support. The Republicans refused to allow the government to increase the amount of debt it could take on unless the health care policy was dropped. Around the world, countries watched with concern as parts of the United States simply stopped working. Can we stop this type of crisis from happening again?

23

A history of ruthless colonial rule and then terrible war have left the Democratic Republic of Congo one of the world's poorest nations.

Poverty Traps

Economic storms may batter developed countries, but those countries are usually rich enough to survive and eventually recover. However, when the global economy is in crisis, whatever the cause, it is the developing countries that are least able to withstand the effects.

Why Rich or Poor?

Qatar has huge reserves of offshore gas and oil, both much-needed energy sources. Other countries import this gas and oil, helping to boost the Qatari economy. The

Democratic Republic of Congo, in Africa, is also rich in natural resources. However, corrupt leaders profited from the resources for their personal gain instead of putting the money into important services such as health, education, and road networks. Some people also believe that the huge multinational companies that try to extract valuable raw materials for profit are also responsible for the corruption that stops the wealth benefitting the general population.

The geographical location of a number of developing countries makes it difficult for them to sustain economic strength. For example, Bangladesh lies on flood plains, and is subject to long and heavy rains that often destroy the country's homes and crops.

LOOK TO THE PAST

Developed countries sometimes lend money to developing countries. In the past, when wealthy countries lent to poorer ones, they charged enormous rates of interest. This meant some countries were never able to pay off their debts. In 2005, campaigners across the world successfully persuaded many governments to cancel the debts of poorer countries. This meant that some developing countries could begin to spend money on essential services such as health care and education rather than spending all their money on interest payments.

The Land Trap

In developing countries, many people in rural areas do not own the land on which they work and live. They may think it is pointless spending money on that land to improve it when they may not be able to stay there. Financial organizations are often reluctant to lend money to people who do not own land or property, because if those people cannot repay the loan, there is nothing the lender can claim back.

Some people argue that lack of ownership of land prevents people in many developing countries from breaking free from poverty.

Fighting, Not Investing

Long civil war or wars with other countries often destroy the road, rail, and air networks that are so important for businesses and farmers sending goods around the world. Political fighting or corrupt governments often prevent an economy from thriving because the politicians involved do not invest in the basic needs of their country, but spend the money on themselves.

Developing Economies

Developing countries often struggle to make an impact on the global economy, and so make life easier for their populations. Although people work hard to try to earn a living, conditions beyond their control often make it very difficult.

The Skills Drain

People from developing countries often leave to find work in another country where there are more jobs and better pay. Often, these workers send money back home to their families. According to the World Bank, the amount sent back is often more than the country receives in aid. However, a country suffers if most of the educated people leave and take their skills with them. Some developing countries such as Haiti and Jamaica hold on to less than 20 percent of their college-educated citizens.

Unfair Trade

Countries can protect their businesses from international competition by placing a tax or charge, called a tariff, on imported goods. Some countries agree not to have tariffs so that global trading is easier and cheaper. This does not always benefit developing countries that produce goods that cannot compete with cheaper goods manufactured by other more developed countries.

Every country needs educated, skilled people to help build and maintain its economy.

Finding a Way to Borrow

In 1976, Mohammad Yunus, an economics professor at the University of Chittagong in Bangladesh, founded the Grameen Bank. Its aim was to lend money over a long term to poor Bangladeshi people to enable them to build their own business, and escape from poverty. The system has successfully helped rebuild many communities, and there are now many other examples of this banking model. However, critics argue that if projects fail, perhaps because of extreme and devastating weather conditions, there can be too much pressure to repay the debts.

COUNTDOWN!

Increased trade across the world creates a demand, often from consumers in developed countries, for cheap, readily available goods. This can lead to serious problems in developing countries, where workers are paid very low wages and face terrible conditions. In 2013, more than 1,000 workers died when a garment factory in Bangladesh collapsed. The building was unsafe, yet many major international stores had used the factory to make clothes to sell all over the world at low prices. Paying workers low wages in unsafe conditions may keep costs down for the consumer and profits up for business, but nothing is worth a human's life and well-being.

Global Meltdown!

How does a problem with the economy in one country cause chaos for another? To understand the causes and effects of economic disaster, we can take a look at the economic crisis that led to the global banking collapse in the early twenty-first century.

Banks were left with "bad debts" when people could not repay their morgage loans. The bad debts affected banks across the world and triggered chaos.

1990s

In the United States, banks encouraged people to take out mortgages to buy their own homes at a low rate of interest. House prices rose. Lenders wanted more people to take out mortgages so they could make more money. They lent to people who were on low incomes and who would not usually have been lent the money. The lenders "sold" the mortgage loans to other banks and investors.

2004-2005

Interest rates began to rise in the United States. Many people were unable to afford the higher monthly repayments on their mortgages. People lost their homes. The banks could not sell the houses because the mortgage payments would be too expensive. House prices dropped. The banks had lent money that would never be repaid, and they had sold these debts on to other banks.

2007

Banks stopped lending to each other, causing a shortage of money. This was known as the "credit crunch." The effects of the credit crunch spread rapidly and sent the world into recession, a situation in which economies shrink rather than grow. Banks would not lend money to businesses, so businesses cut back or stopped operating. People lost their jobs and spent less. This led to more bankruptcies and job losses.

2008

Wall Street bank Lehman Brothers was declared bankrupt. Many other major banks, including three in Iceland, went bankrupt and stopped trading. Britain's central bank, The Bank of England, gave British banks $8 billion to help them recover. The International Monetary Fund (IMF) lent Iceland $2.1 billion dollars.

2009-2010

The G20 Summit—a meeting of the world's 20 most economically powerful countries—approved a $5 trillion injection of money to help the global economy, and agreed to try to better control the activities of banks. The U.S. government gave the Bank of America $20 billion dollars. The global economic crisis hit Eurozone countries such as Greece, Spain, and Portugal.

Lehman Brothers employed 25,000 staff worldwide, and was among the oldest, largest Wall Street investment banks—everyone thought it was too big to fall.

COUNTDOWN!

The complicated network of loans and debts linking banks and other financial institutions partly caused the 2008 economic crisis. Governments promised to figure out the banking system, but there is little evidence that things have changed. Are we just waiting for the next crisis?

Breaking the Banks

Banks are meant to be safe places to keep money. What has brought banks to bankruptcy and the global economy to crisis in recent years?

The Drive for Bonuses

Before the 2008 financial crisis, banks were selling risky packages of debt, such as the mortgages in the United States that were offered to people who could not afford the repayments. People argue that bankers took such risks because they wanted the bonuses that would follow the success of such deals.

Some people believe that the huge salaries and bonuses earned by bankers and traders led them to take too many risks that then contributed the 2008 economic crisis.

Rogue Traders

Investment bankers gamble with huge amounts of money. The traders who buy and sell financial assets work long hours in a highly pressurized environment, often making quick decisions about billion dollar deals. In the recent crisis, some traders, known as "rogue traders," lost large amounts of money, tried to cover up their mistakes, and then lost even more money. In 2008, one of France's largest banks, Société Générale, lost 4.9 billion euros when trader Jérôme Kerviel tried to hide his losses. More recently, the global investment bank JPMorgan Chase lost $6 billion when a trader nicknamed "The White Whale" made risky and dangerous deals, apparently changing bank records to cover up the deals.

SCIENCE SOLUTIONS

Detection

Banks increasingly use software programs to check and analyze traders' accounts and patterns of business to help prevent major losses. Other methods include analyzing a trader's behavior to detect common patterns that occur among rogue traders, such as working particularly long hours and not taking vacations.

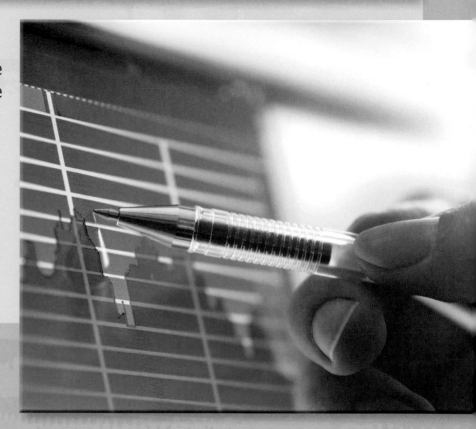

One More Scandal

A new banking scandal was uncovered in 2012. Banks had been fixing, or "rigging," the rate of interest at which they could lend money to each other. This important rate, called London Interbank Offered Rate (Libor), involved billions of deals. Rigging the rate was essentially cheating, to allow some banks to make more money than others.

New Rules for Banks

In 2010, a powerful group of bank regulators from countries around the world, called the Basel Committee on Banking Supervision (BIS), agreed to triple the amount of money that banks must keep to protect themselves against possible losses. This would make sure that savers could be repaid if the banks ran into difficulty. This has been adopted as law in European countries, but, at the time of writing, it remains voluntary in the United States.

Greek protesters demonstrated against job cuts and increases in taxes as the government tried to rescue the country's collapsing economy.

When the Money Runs Out

Financial problems start when we borrow too much money, spend too much money, and get deeper and deeper in debt. This happened to Greece, a country that simply ran out of money.

A Greek Crisis

Greece spent money it did not have and borrowed money to pay for wages, public services, and for big projects such as the 2004 Olympics in Athens. The global economic crisis of 2008 triggered concerns about Greece. Banks worried that Greece would not be able to repay loans. The banks charged even more interest on the loans and that only increased the debt. The Greek government borrowed 110 billion euros from other EU countries and the IMF. The loans came with tough conditions. Greece had to promise to cut back on its spending and get the country into a stronger economic position. The Greek government cut many jobs in education and health care. Teachers, doctors, nurses, and other workers took to the streets to protest.

The Importance of Taxes

In a developed society, education and health care are seen as basic human rights. However, they have to be paid for. Part of the money for these services comes from taxes that are paid by people in work and the businesses they work for. In Greece, the government failed to ensure that taxes owed by businesses and individuals were collected, which meant that they could not then pay for those basic services.

Tightening the Belt

The credit crunch of 2007 led to a shortage of money and a big slump in the global economy. Some governments, such as the coalition government that came to power in Britain in 2010, have since followed an "austerity" program of spending less by cutting back on public services. This has a direct effect on families and individuals. Many people argue that the banks were largely responsible for the crisis so they should be the ones to pay the highest price.

COUNTDOWN!

Detroit, once a giant of the car industry, thrived in the 1950s and 1960s. However, by the 1970s, crises in the oil industry and an increasing number of Japanese car imports hit the U.S. car industry. By 2009, the industry collapsed, bringing down Detroit's economy with it. In 2013, the city was bankrupt. As Michigan governor Rick Snyder said: "Let me be blunt: Detroit is broke." If a once-prosperous city in a developed country can go bankrupt, how many more cities could follow?

Who Is in Charge?

National and local governments are responsible for their national and local economies. Each of these economies is part of a complex network of spending and lending. However, is anyone in charge of the global economy? The simple answer is—no. There are organizations that are responsible for imposing rules and regulations relating to particular parts of the global economy, but it is too big to be controlled by such international bodies. It is up to governments, together with independent organizations, to try to keep the global economy in check.

What Makes the Economy Work?

The problem with keeping an economy healthy is that everyone who contributes to it must agree about how it should be run.

Is a successful economy about setting taxes that are high enough for people to have basic services, or is it about encouraging innovation and new businesses that will offer employment and then encourage

COUNTDOWN!

The financial organization the IMF was set up in 1944 at a UN conference, where 44 governments decided to try to build economic cooperation that would prevent a repeat of the Great Depression. Despite the recent economic crises and agreement among governments to try to prevent future problems, in 2013, the IMF Managing Director Christine Lagarde (left) said, "In far too many countries, improvements in financial markets have not translated into improvements in the real economy—and in the lives of people." She warned, "We are seeing new risks as well as old risks."

The G20 meet every year to review the world economy and establish international policy.

more consumer spending? Different experts and different governments have different views. This makes it difficult for countries to agree on ways to manage the global economy when they come together.

Countries Working As One

The Group of Twenty (G20) is a collection of the world's largest economies, including the United States, Britain, Canada, and Mexico. This group of countries represents more than 90 percent of the global economy. The G20 meet at least once a year to discuss key global economic issues, but each country will also aim to protect the interests of its own population. It can be extremely difficult for G20 members to agree on international monetary policy because each country has its own aims and objectives.

CHAPTER FIVE

A Sustainable Future?

Human activity and population growth put great pressure on our planet's natural resources. One recent **UN** study predicted that the world's population would increase from 7.2 billion to 9.6 billion by 2050. Our planet will need to feed and support that growing population. How can that be achieved fairly around the world when the global economy lurches from one crisis to another?

Much of the world's essential electricity is powered by burning fossil fuels, such as coal, that have a harmful effect on the planet.

Protecting Our Planet

We are using up Earth's natural resources at an alarming rate, which has a serious effect on the environment. We burn huge amounts of the fossil fuels coal, oil, and natural gas, pumping vast quantities of the greenhouse gas carbon dioxide—one of the causes of climate change and global warming—into Earth's atmosphere. Many people argue that there should be a special tax on businesses, called a "green tax," to encourage them to work toward lowering carbon emissions. This would help protect both the communities most vulnerable to climate change and our entire planet.

Electricity for All

According to the International Energy Agency (IEA), 1.3 billion people around the world have no access to electricity. These people live mainly in rural areas in developing countries. The IEA estimates that $1 trillion is needed to provide increased energy access by 2030.

If people in developing countries are to escape from poverty, they need at least some electricity. How will they get the investment needed to improve their living standards?

Forward-thinking Investment

Natural disasters can have a terrible effect on businesses and industry in vulnerable countries. According to a recent UN report, natural disasters have cost the global economy $2.5 trillion since 2000. However, planning for possible disasters can help save millions of dollars at a time. In 2010 and 2011, devastating earthquakes struck New Zealand. The company that owned and ran one of the country's largest electricity distribution networks had already invested $6 million in earthquake protection. This invaluable investment is estimated to have saved the company $65 million.

SCIENCE SOLUTIONS

Fracking

Recent advances in technology have unearthed valuable energy supplies. Hydraulic fracturing, or fracking, is a technique used to extract gas from shale rock deep underground. There are many serious environmental concerns about this technique, but fracking has provided the United States with additional supplies of natural gas, and the country has become an important exporter of the fuel produced. This makes the United States less dependent on imported fuel and so strengthens its economy.

Supporting All the World

Developed countries have grown rich and comfortable, but sometimes at the expense of people in developing countries, and even at the expense of the whole planet. This has serious consequences for the global economy.

Changing Climate

Most scientists agree that human activity has caused climate change, bringing extremes of unpredictable weather, higher temperatures, and melting ice caps. This, in turn, affects what farmers can grow, where people live, and the type of homes they build. If it is left unchecked, climate change will hit the economies of developed as well as developing countries, although the countries that are most vulnerable to the effects of climate change are the poorest.

Feed the World

Around the world, 1 in 7 people—1 billion of the global population—go hungry. Yet, the UN Food and Agriculture Organization (FAO) has stated that we already produce one and a half times as much food as is needed for everyone on the planet to have a sufficient diet. It is not the amount of food, but the way it is distributed and used that causes the problem.

The effect of extreme weather conditions caused by climate change can have a severe impact on local and national economies.

▼

The FAO has produced some shocking figures about global food waste. Each year, 1.3 billion tons (1.2 billion metric tons) of food—one-third of the total produced—is wasted, leading to losses of $750 billion. Producing food that remains uneaten each year uses up as much water as flows along the length of Russia's Volga River. This waste adds 3.6 billion tons (3.3 billion metric tons) of greenhouse gases to Earth's atmosphere, and each year uses up nearly 3.5 billion acres (1.4 billion hectares) of land—28 percent of the world's farmland.

Extreme poverty forces these children in Greece to desperately search for food in garbage dumps.

SCIENCE SOLUTIONS

GM Crops

Weather and pests can destroy a farmer's crops and entire livelihood. Scientists are always trying to discover ways to prevent damage to crops in this way. Advances in science such as genetically modified (GM) crops can help, especially in poor communities, where such technology can help crops succeed, securing a farmer a greater income. However, there is much debate and argument around the use of GM crops. Some people believe they are not safe. Also, multinational companies often provide the technology, so the farmer becomes tied to the company and its conditions.

Since the financial crisis, food kitchens and food banks have become more common in developed countries such as the United States and Britain.

Managing with Less

An economic crisis often leads to a recession. A country's economy shrinks, leading to job losses, little or no increases in pay, and businesses failing. How do countries deal with the effects of a recession? Some cut back on public services. The charity Oxfam suggests that an extra 15 to 25 million people across Europe could be living in poverty by 2025 if austerity programs continue.

What a Waste

We have already seen that there is a huge waste of food in the world, while many people in developing countries are starving.

Our dependence on energy sources such as coal and oil has led to a negative and dramatic impact on the environment. Is it time the developed world used resources more carefully to protect the economic future of all countries in the world?

Americans create 21.5 million tons (19 metric tons) of food waste every year. If that waste was composted, it would result in a massive reduction in greenhouse gas emissions—equivalent to taking more than two million cars off the road!

Recent research suggests that just 90 companies are responsible for nearly two-thirds of greenhouse gas emissions that contribute to climate change. For a long time, the U.S. has been responsible for huge amounts of gas emissions. Countries such as China that now have thriving economies are also responsible for large amounts. However, which countries and governments will take responsibility for addressing the issue of climate change, and tackling the social and economic problems it causes?

Fair Price for All

Around the world, there are organizations to help protect producers of goods in developing countries. The charity Fairtrade, for example, works to make sure that food producers receive a fair price for their goods. They make sure that producers are treated fairly by the large companies, such as supermarkets, that buy their goods. The producers can then build up a long-term business and will receive a good price and treatment for their work.

Paying farmers a decent price for their produce means they can provide for their families and build strong businesses.

LOOK TO THE PAST

In the past, the economy in the developed world has lurched from periods of boom to bust with long-lasting consequences. The economy has been driven by huge energy use from fossil fuels. The effect of that energy use continues to interfere with the planet, from changing climate patterns to the destruction of irreplaceable resources such as rain forests. Billions of people live without access to clean water or enough food. Surely it is time we learned lessons from the past in order to protect the future?

This Is Our World

We may think that we cannot do anything to influence the crises in the global economy. However, there are many actions that individuals and organizations can take—after all, it is our world and it is our economy that are at stake.

Do Campaigns Work?

In many countries, the early 2000s saw new campaigns emerge to tackle poverty, including the Global Call to Action Against Poverty (GCAP) and Make Poverty History. Campaigners called for the governments of developed countries to drop the $1 billion per year of debt repayments that was crippling developing countries. The debt was then dropped for 18 of the countries that had the highest debts.

Direct Action

After the collapse of many banks in the late 2000s, people took to the streets. In 2011, in New York City, a new movement began. It started as no more than a few hundred protesters in a park near Wall Street, New York City's financial district, in September 2011. The protestors were angry that the behavior of banks had led to an economic meltdown, which affected ordinary people most severely. Similar protests followed in other countries. This action became known as the "Occupy movement."

The Occupy movement was a protest against financial inequality around the world.

History Repeats

During the Great Depression in the United States, President Franklin D. Roosevelt talked about the importance of applying "social values more noble than monetary profit." The public reaction to the banks' role in the recent economic crisis suggests that we have not yet learned this lesson. The global economy may generate a lot of money but it is failing to secure decent living standards and a secure future for much of the world's population.

Many people wonder when and if we will learn the lessons from the Great Depression and more recent financial crises. ▶

COUNTDOWN!

We know that climate change has an effect on the global economy, particularly developing economies. We can all help by reducing the amount of energy we use, buying local products, and campaigning for more sustainable energy sources that are less harmful to our environment. We can check that goods we buy are fair trade—thereby ensuring that the producers will receive a fair wage for their products. The actions of many individuals can contribute to significant global change.

Ban Ki-moon, the eighth Secretary-General of the UN, has said that the global economy will need restructuring in order to meet the aims of eradicating poverty and halting climate change.

Can We Win the Race?

About 18 percent of the world's population lives on less than $1.25 a day. In April 2013, the World Bank established a new target. It proposed that by 2030 there should be no more than 3 percent of the world's people existing on only $1.25 a day. This is a hugely ambitious goal because more than 1 billion people still live in extreme poverty.

Global Importance

The global economy matters to everyone. It is not just about multinational companies, banks, and vast amounts of money. The global economy is also about small businesses and individuals. It is about our environment and the future of our planet. It is about confidence in our governments. After all, money is just paper or an invisible bank transaction. Money works only if everyone is confident that the government that produces it can guarantee its value.

Businesses of the World Unite

In 2000, the UN launched the Global Compact—an initiative for world business. According to the UN Secretary-General Ban Ki-moon, "The Global Compact asks companies to embrace universal principles and to partner with the United Nations. It has grown to become a critical platform for the UN to engage effectively with enlightened global business." Businesses can join a voluntary agreement called the UN Global Compact, which sets out 10 aims to encourage businesses to work in a socially and environmentally responsible way. Will this type of voluntary agreement help to keep the global economy from another crisis?

Calling Business to Account

Large corporations sometimes avoid paying taxes by setting up complex financial arrangements in different countries. Recent campaigns have forced some well-known companies to stop avoiding tax payments. Income from taxes helps a nation support its people.

COUNTDOWN!

China is one of the world's largest economies, exporting huge amounts of goods. This booming economy has its disadvantages. China has some of the most polluted cities in the world. It is the world's largest consumer of coal, and second to the United States as a consumer of oil. There are concerns that China's banking system may become caught up in a complex system of loans, similar to the one that triggered the most recent economic crisis. Could problems in China tip the global economy into chaos again?

Glossary

austerity A situation in which a government cuts spending on public services during a recession.

bank A financial institution that holds and invests money, and lends it to businesses and individuals.

bankrupt A term used to describe a company or person unable to repay any debts.

business An organization that produces or exchanges goods or services for a profit.

compost Using food waste as a fertilizer for the soil.

consumer A person who uses a service or buys a product.

currency The money that a country uses, such as the U.S. dollar or British pound.

debt The money that an individual or a business owes to a bank or other financial organization.

Eurozone The area of Europe covered by those EU countries that use the Euro as their currency.

export To sell goods or services to another country.

genetically modified (GM) The process of altering the natural genes (makeup) of food to make growing and harvesting more efficient.

goods Items that are made or sold.

gross domestic product (GDP) The total value of goods and services produced by a country in a year.

import To buy goods or services from another country.

International Monetary Fund (IMF) A worldwide organization that works to make the global economy more stable.

interest Money that is added to savings to increase their value or to a loan to increase the amount of money to be paid back.

interest rate The percentage of interest added to savings or to a loan.

investment Money that is put into a business or financial arrangement in order to make a profit.

mass-produced Made on a large scale.

money Anything that is used and accepted as payment for goods and services.

mortgage A loan with interest added to pay for a home.

producer The person or business that provides goods or services.

production The process of making goods.

profit Financial gain.

raw materials The basic ingredients used for making goods or providing services.

recession When an economy becomes smaller instead of growing.

services Skills offered by a business.

tax An amount of money collected by a government from businesses and individuals.

trade The exchange of goods and services for money or other goods and services.

Further Reading

Books

Anniss, Matt. *World Economy: What's the Future?* (Ask the Experts). New York, NY: Gareth Stevens, 2013.

Economy (Eyewitness). New York, NY: Dorling Kindersley, 2012.

Merino, Noel. *The World Economy* (Current Controversies). Farmington Hills, MI: Greenhaven Press, 2010.

Roome, Hugh and Anne Ross. *The Global Economy: America and the World* (True Books). New York, NY: Children's Press, 2013.

Spilsbury, Richard. *Global Economy* (Hot Topics). Mankato, MN: Capstone, 2012.

Web Sites

Due to the changing nature of Internet links, Rosen Publishing has developed an online list of Web sites related to the subject of this book. This site is updated regularly. Please use this link to access the list:

http://www.rosenlinks.com/WIC/Econ

Index